Our Life in Afghanistan, Pakistan and the United States

A Success Story

Wake Tech. Libraries
9101 Fayetteville Road
Raleigh, North Carolina 27603-5696

Farid**Muti**

Outskirts Press, Inc.
Denver, Colorado

The opinions expressed in this manuscript are solely the opinions of the author and do not represent the opinions or thoughts of the publisher. The author represents and warrants that s/he either owns or has the legal right to publish all material in this book.

Our Life in Afghanistan, Pakistan and the United States
A Success Story

All Rights Reserved.
Copyright © 2008 Farid Muti
V2.0

Cover Photo © 2008 JupiterImages Corporation. All rights reserved - used with permission.

This book may not be reproduced, transmitted, or stored in whole or in part by any means, including graphic, electronic, or mechanical without the express written consent of the publisher except in the case of brief quotations embodied in critical articles and reviews.

Outskirts Press, Inc.
http://www.outskirtspress.com

ISBN: 978-1-4327-1527-4

Outskirts Press and the "OP" logo are trademarks belonging to Outskirts Press, Inc.

PRINTED IN THE UNITED STATES OF AMERICA

CHAPTER ONE
Why I Am Writing this Book

    I wanted to record my ideas and my feelings about my family and Afghanistan and the American people. Since 1991 I have been living in America, in the U.S.A. I was with my father and we were like friends. My father invited me to come with him all the time when he was invited to go to high schools, elementary schools, churches, and universities to speak with Americans. I was always with him during his speeches, and afterward, many Americans asked my father to write a book. I talked with my father and all his American friends and the government; they were happy and they supported us. "You should write a book," they encouraged him. But my father told me, "When I was a professor at Kabul University of Engineering I was standing for eight hours at a lecture. And I wrote many books in Afghanistan, one statistics, two hydraulics, three drafting, and four welding (all engineering books). At that time I was fresh and young, and now I am old and my patience is not like that anymore."

Picture of Father on boat

Farid**Muti**

All my family and friends like Tom Allen, congressman from Maine, Olympia Snow, United States senator, Dr. Richard, president of the University of Southern Maine, Gus Barber, Steve Barber and family, George Campbell, former mayor of Portland, Maine, former governor Angus King, and my neighborhood friends told us that if my father did not feel good and he could not write this book then I could write it. You can see from the next pages that I will explain all the pictures and good stories from our American community during the twenty years we have been living in the United States of America.

Father talking

About My Father's Life

This is a very important section that every friend told us to write in the book. My father's name is Mohammad Hassan Muti. He was born in Heart Province in the city of Kartachar. When he was ten years old he lost his father and mother. He had no sisters. He had a brother who was 18 years old and he was gambling, and the government arrested him and put him in jail. My father was alone with nobody in the house. No electricity. No good water to drink. Half the day he went to school and half the day he worked in a tailor shop and made money to buy food and take care of his life. He worked for two years and he was the top student in his elementary school. And at that time in Afghanistan when he graduated he could have found a job in the government as a clerk, but the headmaster at the school advised my father, "You are very smart, you should continue your education."

Professor Dr. Hassan Muti

My father was interested and wanted to continue his education. At that time the governor of Heart Province was Dr. Zaboli. He talked with my father and told him, "We want to send you to Kabul, the capital of Afghanistan, and you can go to the Afghan Institute of Technology if you pass the test." The Afghan Institute of Technology was newly built and was a partnership between the U.S.A. and Afghanistan, 51 and 49 percent. My father was the top student at his technical school, and his advisors and professors all were Americans. During his school years my father got awards from them. When he graduated, the school and government sent him to the United States for higher education. When he was 19 he went to Wyoming University. He received a BS in civil engineering and professional engineering degree and came back to Afghanistan and earned his master's degree and advanced master's degree.

From Right to left:
my brother Fawad Muti, my father Mohamed Hassan Muti and myself Farid Muti

About My Life In Afghanistan
Before 1978 and the Russians in Afghanistan

I was born in Kabul, the capital of Afghanistan, in an educated family with an open mind. As I remember times were very hard for us and others. When I went to elementary school I walked five miles to school. Our house was on the hill, and the bus stop was two miles away from my house. Most of the time the other students and I would wait to use the city bus to go to school, but the city bus wouldn't stop even though the government law was that for elementary school students, the bus was free.

Our Life in **Afghanistan, Pakistan and the United States**

Kabul, Afghanistan. The Afghan people are very hardworking. They are strong and they build houses on the mountain around Kabul City. My house was halfway up the mountain.

In Afghanistan there were no school buses like in America. Sometimes the bus would not stop for the students. The students would get angry and throw rocks at the bus window and then the driver would stop the car and run after the students and try and catch the one who broke the window. If he caught the culprit, he would find his or her family and make them pay for the damage. The Afghanistan government and police and department of education did not care about this situation.

Our school was a house with twenty rooms. The government made a contract with the owner for the school. The school had no heat and no air conditioning. School started every year on the same day. Our New Year's Day is March 21st. The next day, March 22nd, was our first day of school in Afghanistan. During the months of March and April, because the weather was showers and rain, it was cold, and in class it was very cold. There was no good drinking water in the school. I remember when we were at school with no drinking water it was not good, and many students became dehydrated and sick. The principal and headmaster of the school mixed Patas Parmangate, but the virus was strong and the students got sick.

Farid Muti

Kabul, Afghanistan. I was living with my family at this location and we walked from hill to mountain to go home from school, and other people from work. No civilization existed in this neighborhood.

Before going to school, each student had to fill out an application, so my father and I went to school to get an application for elementary school. My father filled in the form, and one part asked for the leader of the town to sign it as proof of residency. My father and I went to the town leader''s house and knocked on his door. Soon he opened the door. We gave him the form to sign and prove we were living in the town. He went to get his father's signature. Soon he came back and asked us for 100 rupees, which in Afghanistan was equal to two dayswork and salary. Anyway, according to the law there was no charge for the application and signature, but corruption was everywhere. We found out the leader had paid 10,000 to the government to become leader of the town.

I finished elementary school, and at that time when students graduated, the government of Afghanistan and the Department of Education would give a certificate like the one pictured.

In 1959 when my father came back from the U.S.A. and finished the engineering university, he started teaching at the engineering college in Afghanistan. The college was sponsored by Wyoming University, and all the professors were American; my father was the only Afghan professor. During this time he was the assistant director of the Afghan Institute of Technology for three years, and he became general director of all technical colleges at the national level in Afghanistan and the advisor for vocational education and higher education departments in Afghanistan.

During his 35 years of employment, we had a small house in Kabul about ten miles away from the capital Kabul that we built by our own hands. My father was working very hard, and he was very honest, and we have learned a lot from my father, all my family. We are proud of him.

Our Life in **Afghanistan, Pakistan and the United States**

Kabul, Afghanistan

Kabel University

Russian Army in Afghanistan

When the Russians invaded Afghanistan in 1878, life for Afghan people became very hard. Afghan people were not ready for that regime. Afghan ideas were contrary to Russia and its communist regime. Our life became hard and not safe for us to live any longer in Kabul, Afghanistan. Russian soldiers were very angry and had a very bad attitude. When searching people's houses, they would steal the expensive items. Because my father was working with the U.S.A. and teaching at an American college with an American education, twice a month the communist government and Russian soldiers searched our house.

American College of Engineering was shut down from 1978–2000 while Russia was in Afghanistan. The American government opened it in 2001 as Kabul University, which now has more than 9,000 students, 2,800 of whom are women.

My father had a small library and all the books were engineering books. The Russians would check all our house, the books, and each piece of paper. They checked during the morning, afternoon, evening, and even at midnight. When the Russian army and communist government decided to stop all the American schools and colleges, nobody could go to American schools or colleges. They decided they should go to Russian schools and colleges and sent them by force.

When President Dawood signed a contract with Saudi Arabia to build a railroad in Afghanistan, he made a mistake and filled the cabinet with some foolish people. He hired Said Abdullah as his vice president, and the Afghanistans were not happy when President Dawood put communist leaders in jail like Babrak, Karmal, Hatizallah Amin, Noor Mohd Taraki and others. One officer named Assadullah Ahmadzai was teaching in the police academy when President Dawood ordered him to go with more soldiers and bring Noor Mohd Taraki and put him in jail. Assadullah had a German education in police training when he went to Taraki's house and searched it. Taraki's wife was named Cgal Punballatar, and she became the First Lady later on. During the search she was pushed and fell down, and her face started bleeding. She said, "I am bleeding from my face. All Afghanistan will change and bleed like my face. I believe Afghanistan has changed for bleeding." They changed it; the communists changed everything. Education changed from the American system to the Russian system, and American specialists were gone. Afghan people who had American educations like my father and others were replaced from their positions. The communists became one power, president of Afghanistan, vice president, cabinet—all the government officials were Russian under Russian advisors. Russian advisors controlled all operations in Afghanistan.

Our Life in **Afghanistan, Pakistan and the United States**

Kabul - Afghanistan
Top – During the war 1991-92
Bottom today – Defense Department

According to Afghanistan history, Afghanistan has never obeyed a foreign country. Afghanistan has always been fighting. The Afghan people are good people, friendly, faithful, social, and hospitable. They are very hardworking people—my family and I are like Afghan people and American people. A good

9

example is how Afghan people have open houses. It is not necessary to make an appointment to go and see family and friends'. If you are going to visit them at 11:00 in the morning, they don't want to let you go without lunch, and you should eat lunch with them. If you are going at four or five in the afternoon, you will eat dinner with them. Good culture and good customs. Still I obey and respect my customs and culture even while I am in America. I want to ask American people to watch the news and read the magazines to find out from other Americans who spent time in Afghanistan during King Shah and Dawood.

Kochi people moving to a different location. They are moving around Afghanistan trying to stay in a warm place. During all the governments that were in Afghanistan, they never were a problem.

About Our Life in Pakistan

All my family left Afghanistan in September of 1985. We left our house with all the furniture, carpets, refrigerator, and other things. We had very dirty clothes and took the bus with a young guide whose name was Mohd. He had connections with the Mujahideen in the district of Pagman. He took us to Pagman, and we went to a house where a man with his wife and his two kids lived. The guide introduced us to him, and he already knew we were coming. His wife cooked food for us and gave us tea and fruit. The Mujahideen man was working with Mullah Izat, the chief commander of Pagman province. Today Mullah Izat is a businessman in Kabul who made contracts with the government and built Qaunga Pond, hotels, golf courses, and much more. The McDonald's corporation offered Mullah Izat a one-million-dollar contract in Qaunga to open a McDonald's and run the business, but Mullah Izat denied McDonald's because his fighting was not for Russia, his fighting was for business.

Anyway, we walked from Kabul to Pakistan, 300 miles, through mountain and desert with the Mujahideen. It was very hard for all of us. Two times there was fighting between the communities and the Mujahideen, and ten people died. We were walking for weeks. During that time we had no shower and never changed our clothes. We had no good food. Sometimes the whole group walked during the night, all night, because the location was controlled by the communist government and other locations were controlled by the Mujahideen. During the day we were always traveling. For two weeks, we walked. I remember for 24 hours we had no drinks, no food, and all around us was dusty mountain and desert.

Farid**Muti**

Afghan refugees make carpets in their homes by hand and sell them in the city of Peshawar, Pakistan.

The Mujahideen were looking to find a safe place not controlled by the communist government but by the Mujahideen. And when the Mujahideen had a connection in a village, before they entered the village they would contact a spy to find out how the location was. Was it a place to stay longer and relax and stay for lunch and dinner?

It was very hard for everybody for two weeks of walking. During this time, my feet had blisters and sores, and the last day of our travel on the border, all the

Our Life in **Afghanistan, Pakistan and the United States**

Mujahideen and all of us arrived in Paktia, located in south Afghanistan. We were in the village, but there was nobody there. Everybody had left their houses. Most of the houses were destroyed or damaged, and the village government was gone, but on the top of a hill were communist soldiers and their army, and they ordered the Mujahideen and everybody to get out.

Afghanistan

In 1978 the Russian Army invaded Afghanistan. I remember this well. Our house was close to the Kabul airport and the highway. From our location to the airport was about 40 meters of highway. It was Thursday night around six. Cars were coming from the airport to our house. Airplanes were landing at the airport every five minutes. That night was nasty because tanks were crossing, and Babrak Karmal was making a speech on Russian Radio. The army of Russian soldiers went to Qasir Darlaman. The building was built by the first king of Afghanistan, King Amanallah Khan. President Hazizullah Amin was living in this building. The next day the Russian army was all over town and on every street and in each government building. Babrak Karmal was given the power by the Russians to be president of Afghanistan, and Sultan Ali Kishmand was the vice president. They borrowed 1,000 Afghani and at that time they were young and finishing college, and they were ready to go to the army for six months. Hassan Ali Kishmand was older than Sultan Ali Kishmand and he was a classmate with my father at the university in Wyoming. He told my father they were going in the

Farid**Muti**

army and that they didn't have enough money, and if he had 1,000 Afghani could he loan it to them? My father gave them the 1,000 Afghani, and today we are in America and they never have returned my father's money. They became president and vice president. We have, and Afghanistan people have, bad memories from the communist government.

Sardar Dawood was president of Afghanistan from 1972-1978. I remember his son Mirwis Dawood; he had a master's in engineering in electronics from Russia. In 1977 when he came back to Afghanistan with his master's degree, his father told him to go find a job like other people. At that time my father was vice president of the higher educational department in Afghanistan. Mirwis came to my father and talked. After the interview he was eligible to teach in polytechnic built by Russia. Later he told my father, "Dr. Mohammad Hassan Muti, my father is President Dawood and he told me to find a job." Mr. Dawood was a good president and he made a contract with Iran and the Fiat car corporation to build cars in Afghanistan.

Our Life in **Afghanistan, Pakistan and the United States**

In 1993 the communist government was gone, and Freedom Fighters took power in Afghanistan.

During the civil war this building was destroyed – 1991

Kabul 1993

The village wasn't secure because the communist government controlled it—the army controlled it from the hill. Every Mujahideen had a gun, a Klishinkof on their shoulder, and commanded anybody who had a turban to take it off. They wrapped the turbans around their guns and shoulders so the guns didn't 'show. Every two people from our village crossed the border to go to Mangal.

I was with another Afghan Freedom Fighter named Abdul Rahman when he started running away from the village, and I told him not to run. My feet were fine. I was walking. He was running and I started running with him. When I was running, I felt my feet were wet and my socks were wet because of the blisters and sores that had broken but I had no choice at the time. At that moment it was a very hard time for me. Nobody could help and we crossed (God was with us and my family) and we arrived and our travel was done and we went to a hotel, the whole family. When I took off my sneakers, my socks were full of blood.

Tere Mangal was free and not under Pakistan government control. No police, nothing controlled by people and leader and Mujahideen they put their guns and Klishinkof and rockets somewhere in Tere Mangal. I heard they sold some guns and rockets to the border people.

Heart of Afghanistan
Minaret of Heart, Shrine of Gawhar shad Begum on the left side.

About Life in Pakistan

We arrived at the Pakistan border at four in the afternoon, and everybody in our group and all of my family were very tired and all our clothes were dirty after two weeks of no good food, no washing, and no shower. We went to a hotel but it was not a good place. No good bedrooms, no shower, and no good bathrooms, but we spent the night. The next day at 9 a.m. we took a boat from Tere Mangal (the name of the city at the border of Pakistan and Afghanistan). Our trip from Tere Mangal to Peshawar took eight hours. We arrived in Peshawar on September 22, 1985 at 5:30 p.m.

Our Life in **Afghanistan, Pakistan and the United States**

Peshawar City is a big province, and all the people and everybody in the government and schools all speak Pushto. But before the second war it belonged to Afghanistan, and after the second war, the Angris government gave this province (Peshawar) to Pakistan. We call it Durand Line, and Peshawar people were happy to belong to Afghanistan and not Pakistan. Peshawar was a province in Afghanistan; we had an address and our friend's name was Abdullah Duran. He was with his family and they had been our neighbors in Kabul, Afghanistan. We took a taxi. The taxi took us to an Afghan colony in Peshawar and we found his home. We spent a week in his home, and his wife helped us wash our clothes and made dinner and good lunches and breakfasts. During the week we registered our names as refugees in Pakistan with the government there.

When we went to register at the office we took a form. On the form was a fee for the application — (Rs) about five cents. But the clerk asked us for 1,000 Rs, about 50 dollars per application. My father told them the fee for the application was only five Rs and asked why they were asking 1,000 Rs. The clerk told us, "You don't know about life in Pakistan. The thousand rupees are not for me. Everybody wants a share, the director, president, commissioner, and others." Our family gave 6,000 Rs.

Badakhsan River and Badakhsan Province

Afghan refugees, wherever they are in the world, remember their country.

Farid**Muti**

    We spent 300 dollars just to register and get refugee identification, but this identification did not help us find a job or go to college . It did help us with the embassy so others would accept our refugee status like the United States, Canada, Australia, Denmark, Sweden, Germany, France, England, and Norway. This made it very helpful. The countries that helped the most refugees in Pakistan were the United States of America, Sweden, and others. During our stay in our friend Abdullah Duran's house in Pakistan, he helped us a lot, and we want to thank him.

    Afghanistan Ghazni
    A worker sits on the back of a donkey. He is going to find a job.

After a week we found some information about our cousin who lived in Islamabad. Islamabad and Peshawar are 150 miles apart. Early in the morning my friend Abdullah helped take us to the bus station. We took a bus from

Peshawar to Islamabad. From Peshawar to Islamabad it cost 20 Rs (about one dollar per person in 1985; today in 2007 one dollar equals 50 Rs and about 45 Afghani). All my family arrived in Islamabad. We were new to the city and didn't know the location or address. We asked for help from the driver of the bus. He was a good man and he told us to go to a small town just up from Islamabad. Peshawar was a small town but also a big shopping center in the evening where most Afghan people went to shop for groceries and the bakery. When we went to Peshawar and asked others for information about my cousin, they told us that he would be coming in ten minutes.

I waited ten minutes and my cousin with his conductor and ten passengers in a small van stopped at the last destination. My cousin had a BS degree but he couldn't find a job; he was just driving a van. Most of the vans and transportation in Islamabad were driven by Afghan people.

My cousin stopped his car. After there were no more passengers, my family stayed and sat in the van. We went to my cousin's house. He left the station and went out onto the street and was driving when a policeman stopped us. I asked why. There was nothing wrong, so why did he stop us? My cousin told us he talked with him because in Afghanistan, Pakistan, India, Iran, and Bangladesh, when the police stop you, you should get out of the car and talk. So my cousin got out of the car. He went and talked and then came back. He explained that now that we lived in Pakistan, the police wanted money each week. Some wanted 20 Rs. Some wanted 30 Rs and some wanted 40 Rs and some even 50 Rs. I gave him 40 rupees, and we all went to my cousin's house for two weeks.

FaridMuti

Kabul - Afghanistan

Modern building that was damaged during the fighting in Kabul, Afghanistan. In 1991 people moved to a different location to be safe.

Our Life in **Afghanistan, Pakistan and the United States**

During those two weeks, we were looking for a bigger apartment and we found two- and four-bedroom apartments for rent. We made a contract for a three-bedroom place for 1,800 rupees per month with a 100,000 rupee security deposit, which was about 5,000 dollars. On the first floor of the building was a restaurant, butcher shop, video center, printing shop, shoe shop, grocery store, and more. We had a water problem in our apartment and in other apartments because the restaurant took all the water for cooking and washing. But there was no water for us. We talked with the owner of the apartment. He said he would talk with the restaurant owner, but no help came. Over 24 hours, we might have water for half an hour or 45 minutes. During that half hour or 45 minutes, we saved water in the bath, dishes, and gallon jugs. But it wasn't enough. So all the people in the apartment decided to talk with the police. When the police came around and talked with the restaurant owner, there was no help. They took their share and left.

We moved from that apartment to another location, a better apartment. My father had some cash. He told us, "Let's start something, let's start a business or find a job." My father had a PhD in civil engineering from the University of Southern California. First my father applied with the refugee school to teach English, and he told us boys to start a business. We found a good location with busy traffic and a store that was very dirty because it had been a Pakistani restaurant. We made a contract with the owner to pay 3,000 rupees per month and 20,000 rupees as a security deposit, and we opened a billiard club. First we cleaned, washing all walls and floors and the ceiling, doors, and windows. And then painting and remodeling. The billiard business was running well and took care of all our family's needs: the rent of the apartment, the electric bill, and the rent of the shop.

Farid**Muti**

Jawad Muti, my brother, and Jahangir watching two players.

Billiard club members with my brother Jawad Muti in 1991.

At the club there were four tables. Most of the time the tables were very busy and we had good customer service. The first three months the billiard club was open 24 hours a day because we had customers who played.

Professor Dr. Hass Muti with his student in front of a school in Islamabad, Pakistan in 1989.

My father taught advanced English and math for a year but it was not a good salary. Gulbudin Himatyar leader Hezb Islami Afghanistan and Burhanadin Rabani leader Jamiat Islami Afghanistan and Saiant leader Lethat Islami Afghanistan, Subghatullah Myjadidi and Said Ahmad Guilani, another Mujahideen leader—all of these leaders were scared of my father because of his education and experience. He was popular and people trusted him, and also other professors liked my father. Most of them were happy to help their people to have a better life for Afghanistan people. But these leaders gave them a hard time to move to Europe, Germany, France, America, Australia, Sweden, and England. My family applied to come to America. Who was eligible to come to America?
1. If your life was not secure in Afghanistan.
2. If you had an American education (anybody before 1978) or anybody was working with an American corporation in Afghanistan or outside of Afghanistan.

3. If your father or mother was in America they could sponsor their children under the age of 18 or children could sponsor their parents.
4. All of my family came to America.

During the six years in Pakistan, our life was very hard; life was hard for all refugees. Some refugees lived in tents that were very cold during the winter because there was no heat. During summer and spring, there was no air-conditioning, no good medicine, no good water, no good food. Each member of our family was working and went to refugee school. After school and work, we went to the gym for exercise and sport.

Islamabad, Pakistan 1988

Jawaad Muti (second from right) next to his teacher Wahidullah. Young Afghani boys do Tae Kwon Do.

Our Life in **Afghanistan, Pakistan and the United States**

My brother received the high green belt from his teacher Wahidullah. He had a black belt in 1989 in Islamabad. His teacher lived in Canada.

Farid**Muti**

The school where my father taught was supported by Barhanudin Rabani, the leader of Damiat Islami Afghanistan. Barhanudin collected donations for the school from the United Nations. But it did not have good support or pay a good salary, just about the same for four or five months at refugee school as office work, so my father found a better job with Paktel Construction Corporation.

Our Life in **Afghanistan, Pakistan and the United States**

Afghan students under a tent with chairs but no tables. But the families of these students support the school. All Afghan refugees who lived in Peshawar City and Karachi City received help from their relatives living in different countries.

My father was working, and my uncle and aunt were living in Germany. We received every month a check for 300 dollars for support. Everything was very expensive as the Pakistani government had no control.

Farid**Muti**

Farid Muti (March 1986) in Islamabad

    In Islamabad City in September of 1988.
    After three years I left Afghanistan and I was teaching at the Afghan refugee school in Islamabad, Pakistan.
    Afghanistan people respect family values; they obey their culture and their customs even if they live in the U.S.A., Australia, Germany, Canada, England, Denmark, Sweden, or Norway.
    In the picture, from the left, are Farid Muti, Gulam Rabani, who lives in England, and Habibullah, who lives in Canada. They had a video game business in Islamabad.

Our Life in **Afghanistan, Pakistan and the United States**

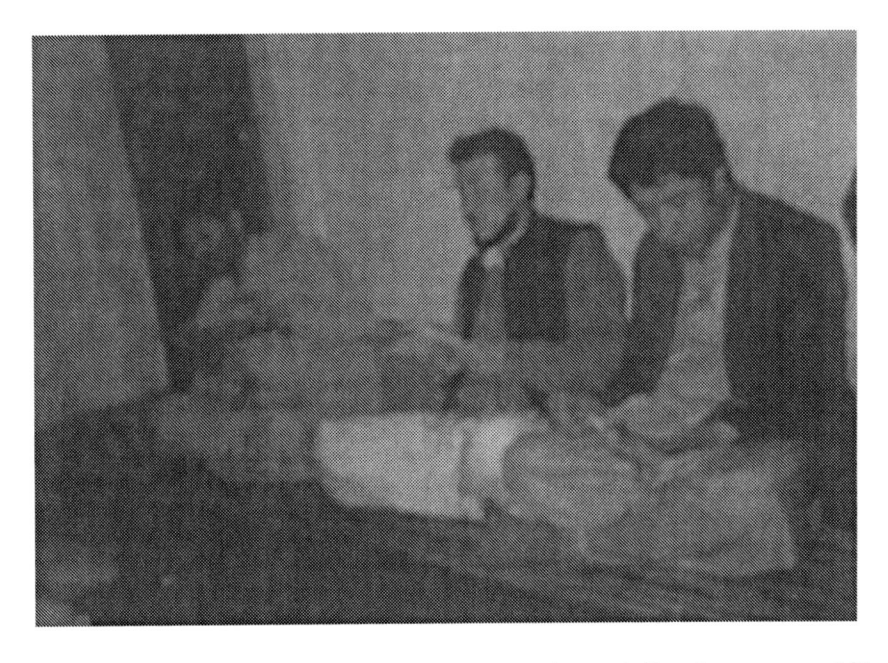

My uncle died. The communist government and Russian army killed him in 1989 in Afghanistan. We pray for him in Islamabad.

1989 in Islamabad.

Malam Qadir, on the right, lives in Australia, and Baqir lives in Afghanistan and, at left, Mohd Sharif lives in Germany. We pray for my uncle; we celebrate and pray in 1989.

My uncle's name is Homayoun Salemy. In June 1987 he came to visit us in Pakistan. When he arrived at the airport, he had a German passport and German citizenship, but the airport employee asked for his share. My uncle gave him 200 deutsche marks, the equivalent of 150 US dollars. All of us in the family were at the airport to welcome him. It had been nine years since I had seen my uncle. He left Afghanistan with my other uncle and aunt in 1978 when Russia invaded Afghanistan. My uncle and aunt were very kind and good people. They helped us in Pakistan.

Once when my uncle was in Pakistan he tried to drive a car. He was thinking that it was like in Germany—everything by law is good. He couldn't drive for ten minutes. One evening friends and family were visiting my uncle, and we had guests in our house. Some cops came, knocked on our door, and came inside our house. We asked them, "What are you doing?" They told us they were searching our house. I asked them if they had an order from the court and they said, "No." They checked our house but they couldn't find anything. They told all of us to go to the police station. We all went to the police station. My father spoke English with the sheriff and the chief. After ten minutes of communication, the police chief and sheriff told us sorry, that it was a mistake and they were sorry to bother our family. So we came back home.

After one month, from June 1987 to July 1987, my uncle went back to Germany. When he arrived home, my uncle and aunt sent my mother, my sister, my father, and my brothers a gift parcel. The post office didn't deliver it to our house; the postman knocked on our door and gave us a note that said to come to the post office and pick up a parcel. The next day I told my mother and father that I would go to the post office to pick it up. My father said, "Can I go with you?" I said, "Yes, Father, you can go." When we went to the post office it was a general office. We went to the clerk, who brought our parcel from the back and opened it—inside was shampoo, soap, aftershave, shaving cream, hair spray, and other items. It was a small parcel and the clerk told us to pay 1,000 rupees. My father started speaking in English, saying, "Why a thousand? This is a small parcel and gift. This is not for business." The clerk said that everyone wanted a share, but we could go and talk with the general manager on the third floor, Room 345. I went with my father to the general manager's office. His secretary gave us permission and we went inside. First, my father explained to the general manager about the parcel. He said, "This is the law." My father said, "Show me the law, on paper." The general manager asked my father where he learned to speak English. "You speak English very good and perfect." My father told him that he had studied in the United States of America. The manager was interested to talk more with my father about Afghanistan and politics. He asked my father what he had done when he was in Afghanistan. My father told him that he taught engineering and was the advisor for the vocational and educational department in Afghanistan. This made the general manager change. He opened a book and checked how much tax we should give. The book said 98 rupees, which we paid, and we received our parcel. The general manager took three bottles of shampoo and aftershave. My father and I left the general post office and came back home.

My father found a job with Paktel Construction Corporation in Islamabad (part time) and he made contact with Mr. Khalil, General Managing Director. He provided housing for 1,000 families between Peshawar and Islamabad. My father designed sewer plane machines for them, designed completely, and the government accepted them. So they gave a contract to my father.

The second project contract was in 1990 in December, and the project was

Our Life in **Afghanistan, Pakistan and the United States**

in Islamabad. My father very quickly completed the design for the general managing director of Paktel Construction. But they didn't give my father a contract for that design. My father told him that as soon as their program was done that we were going to America. The director told my father that he had no money to give him. My father could not do anything, even though this project involved powerful people like former president Ziaullag's son and Nawaz Sharrif. We came to the States and they didn't give my father his salary.

When I was in Pakistan from September 1985 to December 1991, life was not secure for all Afghan people. If people lived in Pakistan or Saudi Arabia, Kuwait refugee people could not buy houses, get permanent residency, go to college, or get good jobs. Everything was very expensive, especially rentals. Afghan families who lived in Islamabad had to pay security deposits one year in advance, six months in advance, or a deposit of 20,000 rupees (which equaled 1,500 US dollars, or one year's salary for a full-time job in Pakistan).

If relatives and members of the family didn't help from the United States, Germany, France, Sweden, Australia, Canada, Denmark, Norway, or England, it was very hard for Afghans to give the advance security for rental apartments.

According to Afghan people, it was very hard in Russia. Some Afghan people or communists went to Russia when the Taliban took power in Afghanistan and the Mujahideen took power in Afghanistan. Life was hard for them. In Russia the salary for Russian people was good. An engineer with a master's degree or PhD got a salary every month between 200 or 300 rubles. If they wanted to buy a house or a car, they filled out an application and in two or three years they'd get a house or car. For Afghan refugee people, they increased rental apartments to 300 or 400 dollars a month, which was six month's salary in Russia.

When I was in Pakistan, the Afghan people received letters from members of their family or relatives, and I collected stamps from the different countries: the United States of America, England, Canada, Germany, France, Australia, Sweden, Norway, Mexico, Cuba, Uganda, Kenya, India, Romania, and Sudan. The most helpful countries for Afghan refugees in Pakistan were the United States of America, Canada, Sweden, France, Australia, Denmark, England, and organizations like the American Red Cross, United Nations, and UNDP. Each of the above helped with health, education, and employment. If Afghan people worked with them, they gave them jobs. People could receive help and letters from their family and relatives from each of these countries. You can see each country's stamp; some stamps are 25 to 30 years old. Twenty-eight years ago, when I was with my family as refugees in Pakistan, we received help from Germany because my uncle lived there. More than 25 of our relatives live in Germany.

Afghan refugee people lived in Hamburg. Some of them got permanent residency and some didn't. I hope the German government will accept more applications from Afghan refugees.

After 1986, the policy of the United States changed about who was eligible to enter the United States of America. Anyone who had an American education and worked with an American corporation before 1978 could come. Before 1978, Russia invited Afghanistan people.

Parents who lived in the United States and had children under 18 or were single could sponsor them. The United States of America helped Afghanistan, before the communist government, with education, economy, business, and a better life for Afghan people. Afghanistan people and Afghanistan government had a strong friendship with American people and American government. When the communists took power in Afghanistan, all the American diplomats left Afghanistan. They came back to the United States of America in 1978.

Afghan refugees left Afghanistan and went to Pakistan and contacted the US embassy. After completing the application process, the United States of America government accepted their application to permanently live in the United States. Now our Afghan people are working well with government, business, and corporations; they have bought houses and cars, and they have good jobs.

Our friends received letters of help from the U.S.A. Family and friends who lived in America sponsored other friends and family. People got education in the States or worked with American corporations so they were eligible to come to the United States for work and life. Since 1978, about a half a million Afghan people have come to the United States, mainly to California, Virginia, New York, Maine, Boston, Chicago, North Carolina, New Jersey, New Hampshire, Connecticut, Arizona, Texas, Philadelphia, Delaware, Florida, Miami, Washington, Rhode Island, Maryland, Iowa, Ohio, South Carolina, Kentucky, and Georgia.

Afghan refugees received letters of help from their relatives and members of their family, and the Canadian government helped with education. For Afghan refugees living in Pakistan, the Canadian government opened English courses taught by Canadian teachers. When students completed the course they received certificates.

Afghan refugees received letters of help from their family members and relatives. Also, when Afghan students in Kabul had been to French schools in Afghanistan and finished college in France before 1978, the French government would sponsor them to live and study in France.

People received letters of help from members of their family and relatives.

Our Life in **Afghanistan, Pakistan and the United States**

Afghan people lived in India, but they received help from the United Nations. Each person who was an Afghan refugee received 800 rupees every month. In 1990 when I was an Afghan refugee in Pakistan, one dollar = 30 rupees and 800 rupees = 24 dollars. Every month 800 rupees was one month's salary and labor.

Afghan refugees in Portland, Maine airport.

The refugees were welcoming an Afghan family of refugees coming from India and Pakistan in 1993. When we come to the U.S.A., UK, Germany, France, Canada, Sweden, Norway, and other countries, we should remember our people, how they are living.

In Germany, some Afghan people live in cities like Hamburg, Frankfurt, Munshon, Kagal, and others. They apply to become permanent residents, but the German government denies their application. They have lost their jobs, their houses, left everything behind them in Afghanistan. I am writing this book for the German government and other countries like Germany to help their Afghan refugees and accept their applications to live and work permanently.

different countries, and they lost their houses, their jobs; everything got left behind. First Afghan refugee people went to Germany by flying from India and Pakistan and other ways. When they arrived in Germany, before landing, they destroyed all their documents, such as passports and tickets, by putting them in the toilet. When they went to the German airport in Frankfurt or Hamburg, immigration processed their applications, and their applications were approved. They then sponsored their families.

Most Afghan refugee people lived in Iran. Their language is similar to Afghanistan; their culture is the same. Iran people speak Farsi, and Afghanistan people speak Farsi, Pushta, Uzbaki, and Tajeki. More than two million refugees were living in Iran from 1978 to 2001. After the Taliban and communist government's regime, most of them went back to Afghanistan. Always the Iran people and Iran government showed friendship and provided economic, educational, and agricultural assistance. When President Dawood was president between 1972 and 1978, the Iran and Afghanistan governments had an agreement and contract. Afghan workers and some college students could go to Iran and work to support their families. During the communist government's administration, Iran helped Afghan refugees, and two million Afghan refugees lived in Iran.

Sweden helped Afghanistan when Russia invaded Afghanistan. Afghan refugees in Pakistan received help from the Swedish committee for Afghanistan in Peshawar, Pakistan. Their head office was in Peshawar. Swedes helped with education, health, and construction. Thank you to the Swedish government and the Swedish people

Farid **Muti**

Afghan people also lived in Czechoslovakia. During the communist government's regime, they went for an education and stayed in Czechoslovakia, but the country did not accept refugees. When Dr. Najibullah was president of Afghanistan and then when Babrak Karmal was president, the Afghan communist government sent more than one hundred students a year for higher education. Some of it was good, but right now I do not have enough information on the Czechoslovakian government.

When our first King Amanullah Khan was in power, the flag had three colors:

1. Black: dark, not peaceful
2. Red: blood, fighting with anger
3. Green: peace and freedom

This picture was taken in July 1987 in Pakistan at an Afghanistan refugee camp. All refugees helped each other prepare Afghan kabobs to sell at the market and restaurants. Most of these people had finished college and high school in Afghanistan, but when they applied for a job with Pakistani corporations or the government, their applications were always rejected

Bamyan

The large Buddha, 180 feet high, is carved in the face of the cliff. Every year thousands of tourists from many countries come to see the Buddha sculpture. It is

Darulaman Palace was designed as the new capital city by King Amanullah in 1923. During the communist government's administration, when Hafizullah Amin was president of Afghanistan, he lived in the big house. When the first Russian army attack happened, he was killed in the building. When Babrak Karmal was made president by the Russians, this building was the defense department.

Kabul-Bagh-e-Bala is a graceful and many-domed palace that glimmers on a hill to the north of the city. It was built by Amir A. Rahman (1880–1901) as a summer palace. He died there. During the fighting in Kabul, it was destroyed but again, with American help, was rebuilt and opened for the public to swim and go to the hotel. People can hold their weddings and parties there.

Mazar Sharif Mosque in Afghanistan. Every year on March 21st people from all around Afghanistan come to pray and hang Janda — the good news. On this day, March 21st, people were lost and could not see and couldn't walk. Then, that day, some of them were at this mosque and their eyes were opened, and they could see again and others could walk again. People from all over

Afghanistan, Sudan, Bangladesh, and Pakistan during the first day of the new year's celebration travel to Mazar Sharif. People who are sick, mute, or alone will be cured.

Buzkashi

Buzkashi is a game played on horseback, a very physical game, where each player is a heavyweight champion and must pull a sheep that is about 150 to 200 pounds. As they pull the sheep, they try to get it in the middle of the circle to be the winner. Not just any horse can be used; these are very special horses, very expensive. Every year all these champion horse runners — Buzkashi — travel with their horses to different cities in Afghanistan and perform their sport.

The Afghani government and the United States have been friends since 2001. When the Russian army invaded Afghanistan, all the diplomats of the U.S.A., England, Germany, France, Australia, Canada, Sweden, Norway, Holland, Denmark, and the United Nations left Afghanistan. They went back to their countries, and Afghanistan was left in the hands of Russia. Life with the Russians was hard. The American School, like the Afghan Institute of Technology and Engineering Faculty, was sponsored by Wyoming University. The communist government of Russia decided to close these colleges, saying that students should go to the Russian School and learn the Russian language. Since 2001 and into the present, the United States has supported Afghanistan. We appreciate their support, but we need more support from Europe and other countries to help our education. In order to help the Afghanistan economy and provide jobs with good salaries, the United States opened a university in Darulama Kabul, Afghanistan, named the American University at Kabul, Afghanistan. This is the second university the United States has opened in Asia. The other is the American University at Beirut.

I am not happy with the Boon Conference because they chose inexperienced people for the cabinet, people who have never been a clerk and don't know about management, who the leader is, or even how to be a leader. Not everyone can be a leader. Afghanistan needs a good leader who can provide housing, health benefits, education, and jobs with good salaries.

Mr. Karzai is a good man. He has a good attitude and personality. However, he is not a strong leader. If he was a strong leader, then the United States and NATO would have supported Afghanistan in 2001. Afghanistan shouldn't live with suicide bombs every day. I am asking the Afghani parliament and senators who sit in parliament on behalf of their people to go to their state and talk with their people and ask what they want. Some people in parliament cannot write their names or think well. Today in Afghanistan, there are between 30 to 50 women in parliament. Most senators like to drive Land Cruisers and have drivers. I am asking Karzai to bring good people into parliament and the cabinet.

Afghanistan has good education for its people. Some of them have master's degrees or PhDs from the United States, England, Germany, and France. They have management and leadership experience in government. Mr. Karzai should invite them to help. Otherwise, Afghanistan will not be a place for education and honest, hardworking people. I know people who give training for Karzai and his cabinet and parliament. The American army and NATO tell him how he should control the Afghani government to give the Afghani people safe and good lives. Today the Karzai government is corrupt. He is happy for the corruption. He was born for corruption. His life was full of corrupt people, and he followed these corrupt people. Why doesn't the Boon Conference ask Karzai and his cabinet what kind of government they are running? The Boon Conference should make better decisions.

I am asking Karzai and his cabinet and parliament to look at these boys.

The weather is cold. They don't have good clothes or warm clothes or warm shoes. Still you are ignoring how people live in Afghanistan. These boys need to go to school. They need clinics. They told me, *We don't know the government, any government coming. They are not working for us. They are working for themselves. God help us. God is with us.*

Look at these boys again.

Their hands and feet show that during a month they have showered once or twice because there wasn't enough water. They are interested in going to school. But there is no school in their town, no hospital, no good medicine for when they get sick.

This is the house of the Afghani president. King Zahir Shah was living here, and now Karzai lives and works here, like the White House in the United States. This building is located in Kabul, Afghanistan with more than five acres of land.

CHAPTER**TWO**
Life in the United States of America

On December 19, 1991, my entire family traveled from Pakistan to Germany, and from Germany to the United States. Our last transit was in New York, and our sponsor office was the Refugee Resettlement Program in Portland, Maine. We spent a night in New York. The next day we traveled by United Airlines to Portland. When we arrived, our case worker was there waiting for us. Her name was Ellen McKenzie. She brought a big van for all my family and our luggage. She took us to an apartment. During the first three weeks, our social security was processed and we had medical checkups. When we finished, we began looking for jobs and going to school. My brothers and I found jobs at Barber Foods. First we started as temporary workers at Barber Foods, and after a month we were given full-time jobs. We worked there for ten years. In 1997, I was named Employee of the Month.

After a year's work at Barber Foods, my family decided to buy a house in Portland, Maine. On our second day at our new house, my father got a phone call from Mike Clarke at Channel Eight News, WMTM. The government chose us because of good family values and good attitudes.

One year when I was working at the Barber Food Industry, I received a birthday card. My birthday was on the Fourth of July. On the card was the signature of Steve Barber, the president of Barber Foods. I had never met him. One day, a young man was walking around the production line and watching us and talking with the supervisors. I asked my trainer who he was. My trainer told me that he was Steve Barber, the president of the company. I went and told him thank you for the birthday card and I shook his hand. The Barber family is very kind. They are good people and help people get a job and find their way. Mr. Barber was an immigrant from Armenia.

At the Campus Center of the University of Southern Maine on June 14, 1996. From left to right, Dr. Richard Pattenaude, President of the University of Southern

Farid**Muti**

and Northern Maine, Farid Muti, student at the university, and Steve Barber, president of Barber Foods Industry.

Every year Barber Foods celebrates summer with a picnic in Portland, Old Orchard Beach, or Sebago Lake. This picture was taken in June of 1997 at Sebago Lake. From left to right, my father Mohamed Hassan Muti, university professor, Marjorie Barber, chairman of Barber Foods, Julie Barber, director of marketing, Kathy Barber, management program director, Gus Barber, chairman of Barber Foods, and my mother, Salena Muti.

I have a good memory still in my mind. Good luck.

Picture Barbers Father

When the Russian army invaded Afghanistan in 1978, life became insecure for millions of Afghan freedom lovers. Since my family's life was in danger in

Our Life in **Afghanistan, Pakistan and the United States**

Afghanistan, we had to escape to Pakistan, leaving all of our property behind. On December 1991 we came to Portland, Maine. As refugees through the Refugee Resettlement Program, with their help, three of our family members were employed. When we were in Afghanistan and Pakistan, every member of the family worked at home and outside the home as much as they could. Through working, our family was economically independent.

When we came to the United States, we knew about the American work ethic. My father always insisted on our proper conduct and good behavior at work. During our first two years at Barber Foods, my two brothers and I got along very well with everyone. Finally our family decided to settle in Portland, and on January 27, 1993 we moved into our own house. In our family, six of the eight family members were working at permanent or temporary jobs. Our economical problems were solved, and we enjoyed life through hard work.

CHAPTER THREE
American Freedom and Prosperity

In February of 1993, anchorman Mike Clark from Channel 8 made a film about the lives of refugees in Maine and New England. Our family was chosen for a TV interview.

From left to right. Professor Muti, anchorman Mike Clark, Bill, real estate broker, cameraman Channel 8.

Farid**Muti**

Pic of tea

On September 23, 1993, a very lovely Thursday I will remember, my family received this invitation:

> The Maine Refugee Advisory Council Requests the Honor
> Of your presence at a Blaine House Tea to celebrate the
> Diversity among Maine's Refugee Communities.
>
> Thursday, September 23, 1993 at 2:30 pm
> The Blaine House Mansion
> 192 State Street
> Augusta, Maine
>
> P.S. Please plan to stay with us for the 3:30 presentation
> by Maine Senate President Dennis Dutremble

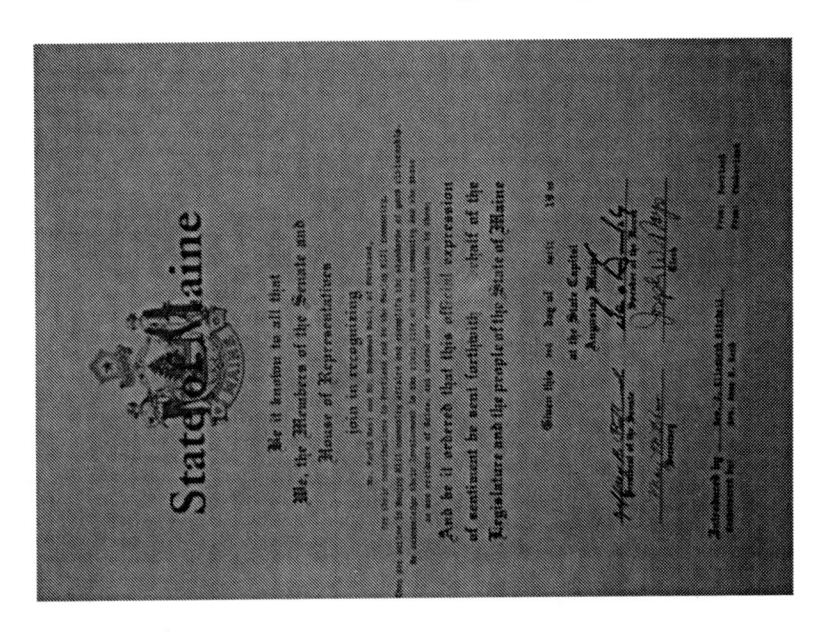

Our Life in **Afghanistan, Pakistan and the United States**

The Muti family received this award from the governor in 1996

April 1996. On a fresh, sunny day in Portland, Maine, the Munjoy Hill neighborhood association held the annual meeting at 7 p.m. The meeting was at the community building, the big building. About 500 people attended, and many people received awards, and at the end of the meeting, State Senator Ann Rand and State Representative Elizabeth Mitchell, president and speaker of the house, announced they had a special announcement and a special award. First the senator read my father's biography, and then both women invited me and my father to receive a special award from the Maine people and the governor. We were very happy to receive this award.

Farid**Muti**

Front from left: Mary Dime, Senator Ann Rand, Marge Niblock, Fawad Muti, Gary M.

In January of 1997 I applied for United States citizenship, and after checking my employment, background, and passing a test, I received my citizenship in August of 1997 in Kennebunk, Maine. Congressman Tom Allen was present and greeted me warmly.

Congressman Tom Allen says congratulations to Farid Muti (United States citizen)

There were newspaper reporters and Channel 8 news attending the citizenship ceremony. Many immigrant people from different countries were at the naturalization ceremony, including people from Afghanistan, England, Sweden, Norway, Cambodia, Pakistan, Bosnia, Romania, Bulgaria, France, Vietnam, Poland, Eritrea, Ethiopia, Korea, Canada, India, China, and Russia. Every year 5,000 Russians come to America.

Our Life in **Afghanistan, Pakistan and the United States**

Everyone had to sit on a numbered chair and wait for their name to receive their naturalization certificate.

Farid Muti, in line, waiting to take a number and go inside Town Hall in Kennebunk, Maine for the ceremony in June of 1997.

Farid**Muti**

Andrew Young, former American ambassador to the United Nations and friend. On the left, Farid Muti at Pavilion Club in Portland, Maine.

In June of 1997, when I received my United States citizenship, the Maine government and Department of Immigration and Naturalization decided to pick someone to interview on TV and in the New England newspapers. On Tuesday, July 1, 1997 at 5 p.m., I received a call from the Portland newspaper. Staff writer for the *Portland Press Herald*, Sarah Ragland interviewed me on the phone for 20 minutes, and she asked to take pictures and interview me at home with my family. She came the next day at 5 p.m. to take our picture and complete the interview. Finally, on July 4, 1997, our interview was in the *Portland Press Herald*. When my interview appeared in the paper, I received congratulations from friends in Portland, Maine, Massachusetts, and New Hampshire. But, to my surprise, I received postcards from people I didn't even know, and I still have not met them. I want to say thank you to Maine people, Channel 8 news, and the Maine government for helping us and supporting all of my family.

Our Life in **Afghanistan, Pakistan and the United States**

Channel 8 news WMTV and my three brothers outside of Kennebunk Town Hall, Maine for an interview in June, 1997.

In June, 1997 my teacher at the University of Southern Maine, Bo Hewey, Kristina Hewey, Valerie, Priscilla Green, Executive Director for Senior Citizens in the State of Maine, and Terry Foster, Director of International Students for the University of Southern Maine, came to our house to say congratulations.

A special notice and congratulation from Bill Clinton, President of the United States of America. In June of 1997 in Kennebunk, Maine at 3 p.m., every immigrant received congratulations from the President when they became American citizens. I want to say thank you to Bill Clinton, President of the United States of America from 1992–2000.

My advice for all immigrants and refugees that have lived in the United States of America for at least five years and have a green card is to apply for United Statescitizenship. When they become citizens of the United States of America, they can work with the government, they can sponsor their family, and they can vote. They can even get a government position. When I received my citizenship, for three years I was on the Board of Directors for the city of Portland, Maine, and the city of Portland has 70,000 people in its population. A good example is Arnold Schwarzenegger. He was an immigrant and today he is the governor of the state of California. Another good example is Congressman Obama, who came from Alabama to Washington, DC; he is from Indonesia and he wants to become the president of the United States of America. Another example is my father. For six years he was the commissioner of civil service for the city of Portland, Maine. Also, he taught at the University of Southern Maine.

By the time I became a United States citizen, I applied to sponsor my fiancée from Pakistan. She had been living with her family as an Afghan refugee for five years. A very happy moment in my life was when I brought her over to the United States. In fact, with the help of our good friend Tom Allen, congressman, and also his district director, Mark Ouellette, she came within three months. We got married in the United States in Portland, Maine in 1998. Now my family is growing, and we have two wonderful kids and have a secure and happy life together.

CHAPTER **FOUR**
Life in Afghanistan

As I was watching the Channel 9 news from Virginia, live from Washington, DC and again later on CNN News, George W. Bush, President of the United States, spoke about Afghanistan's people. His speech was for the American people as it relates to the aftermath of September 11th. He stated that the Afghanistani's are good people, and how we should help and give them respect. After September 11, life for Afghanistan people was different. Some had businesses and were attacked by hungry people. Some of them couldn't find jobs for some time. When I heard President Bush make a statement about Afghanistan's people, I sent a postcard to him at 1600 Pennsylvania Avenue in Washington, DC. It said:

"Mr. President, I like your speech when I was watching the News on Channel 9, CNN News about Afghan people. Afghan people are good people and we should look to them with respect. We should help them." I addressed my postcard to read: "My postcard to the President of the United States."

I sent some pictures to President Bush after 2001 when the Taliban destroyed and exploded in 2001 in Bamyan, Afghanistan, November 16, 2001 at 2:30 p.m.

I opened my mail box to collect my mail and I saw a packet from the White House in Washington, DC. I opened the envelope to find a card and the signature of President George W. Bush. We were surprised to receive the card from the President.

"Thank you for writing about the act of war committed against the United States on September 11th. In the face of this evil, our country remains strong and united, a beacon of freedom and opportunity to the rest of the world.

"Our government continues to function without interruption. Our intelligence, military, and law enforcement communities are working non-stop to find those responsible for these acts. We will make no distinction between the terrorists who committed these acts and those who help harbor them.

"We must remember that our Arab and Muslim American citizens love our nation and must be treated with dignity and respect. Americans of every creed, ethnicity, and national origin must unite against our common enemies.

"Since these terrible tragedies occurred, our citizens have been generous, kind, resourceful, and brave. I encourage all Americans to find a way to help. Web sites like libraryunites.org can serve as a resource for those wanting to participate in the relief efforts.

"I deeply appreciate the support and prayers of so many Americans. God bless you and your family, and God bless America!"

From me and my family: Thank you, Mr. President, government, and American people, for helping my family have a better life and better education and for the Afghanistan government and Afghan people who live in the United States or Afghanistan.

I moved from Maine in October 2000 to Virginia. I couldn't find a job quickly. I was searching to find a job but no one called for interviews. It was very hard for me. I was unemployed and received unemployment from the State of Maine.

From 2000-2002 I was unemployed. I was thinking about talking with our family friend and my father's friend, Congressman Tom Allen. I talked with him, and he gave a good recommendation but no good results came. Because my first name was Ahmad.

I filled out applications, with good employment background and references. But no reply. I contacted companies about my application, but still, no reply. Two employers called me after receiving the recommendation from the congressman from Maine. Employers told me, Okay, we want to keep your application on file. But no interview and no job.

Congress of the United States House of Representatives, Washington, DC

November 14, 2001

To All Potential Employers:

I am writing on behalf of friend and former constituent, Mr. Farid Muti. Mr. Muti has asked that I write a letter of support for him, and I am delighted to do so.

I came to know Farid and his family through my Congressional office and campaign. During his time at Barber Food in Portland, Maine. Farid received recognition for his work and by all accounts was an exceptional employee on my campaign. He performed several tasks and could always be counted on to be punctual and helpful.

In greater Portland, the Muti family have become tireless advocates for immigrants. Farid, when he was here, served on several boards and become a strong community advocate in his own right. He was and remains a high-rated citizen. I expect Farid will be an outstanding employee in whatever field he pursues.

I trust you will give him every opportunity to prove himself.

Sincerely,

Tom Allen,
Member of Congress

Farid**Muti**

University of South Maine
Office of the President
June 14, 1999

Mr. Farid Muti
65 Mount Fort Street
Portland, ME 04101

Dear Farid Muti:

Thank you for the wonderful invitation to dinner with you and your family Friday night. It was an honor to be asked and I enjoyed myself immensely. The food was superb and the company was stimulating. I was honored to meet your mother and father. You and your family should be extraordinarily proud of what you have accomplished in the United States. Your family is a model for others who strive to come here and struggle to be successful. Over the years ahead, you and your family will be assets of great value to our community. Again, thank you for the delightful dinner.

Sincerely,

Richard L. Pattenaude, President

University of South Maine
Office of the President

March 4, 1997

Mr. Farid Muti and Family
65 Mount Fort Street
Portland, ME 04101

Dear Farid Muti:

What a wonderful feast. I want to thank you, your mother, and your family for their most generous and tasty gift. The lunch was excellent and everyone on this floor of the building enjoyed it very much. We are most thankful.

I look forward to the opportunity to meet with you and your father to talk about education and other issues. Until then, you have my best wishes and, again our sincere thanks.

Sincerely,

Richard L. Pattenaude, President

Farid**Muti**

United States Senate
Washington, DC 20510

Olympia Snowe
Maine

April 12, 2000

Dear Farid Muti & Mrs. Muti:

I am so happy to join your family and friends in welcoming Sarah into the world. I know this is an exciting time for all of you.

It is always nice to hear about happy, healthy babies being born into such wonderful and loving families. I am very happy for you.

Sincerely,

Olympia Snowe
United States Senator

Olympia Snowe, United States Senator, and Farid Muti (in Portland, Maine).

On the left is my house, 206 Congress Street, Portland, ME U.S.A. Congress and the Senate are working hard to bring something better for their people and their towns in the United States. People give them their votes, and they work hard for the people. But our senators and congressmen in Afghanistan are going to the office and home, and they are not thinking about Afghanistan and the people. We should learn from America.

Our Life in **Afghanistan, Pakistan and the United States**

4B *Portland Press Herald*, Friday, June 14, 1996

Munjoy Hill Group Opens Its Arms to All

From Staff Report

All geographic boundaries were eliminated from the bylaws at the Munjoy Hill neighborhood organization during the group's annual meeting Tuesday. Until now, only residents on Portland's Munjoy Hill could be voting members or serve on the organization's Board of Directors.

"The push for change started as a proposal to expand the traditional boundaries at Munjoy Hill beyond Washington Avenue to include the East Bayside neighborhood. But since Tuesday's decision, we have dropped all boundaries," said Cynthia Fitzgerald, the group's secretary. "You always could join but now everybody that joins will have voting rights. We are going to let it go from there and see what develops. Even people who live outside Portland are welcome to join." The organization also honored seven people with its annual Good Neighbor Awards, including Mohammad Muti, a refugee from Afghanistan, who is a leader in Portland's immigrant community. New board members are Farid Muti, Edward Rosenthal and Joan Gauche.

The Munjoy Hill community is located in Portland, Maine with 20,000 houses and a very strong community in Maine. On the board of directors, all were very involved. Every member of the community was interested in joining the meeting. When Hilary Clinton came to Portland, Maine in 1997, the Munjoy Hill community was ready to set up meetings for 500 people at the community center. I couldn't find a good job to take care of my family. First, I moved from Virginia to North Carolina with my wife and two daughters, who were staying at a relative's home.

Trip to Afghanistan after 20 years

When we arrived at Kabul Airport to claim our luggage, it had not yet arrived, so we filled out paperwork so that when the luggage came the next day, we would be notified. The next day came but they could not find our luggage. For two or three weeks they couldn't find our luggage. Also, the airport couldn't deliver missing luggage to any address. Sometimes passengers lost once in Kabul City, the capital of Afghanistan. Kabul had a huge population from all around Afghanistan. The people originally living in Kabul all left as refugees to America, Europe, Canada, and other countries.

If you are driving around the city in light traffic, the government controls their traffic. They hire a police officer to stand at the four-way to control the traffic and traffic lane, with people driving in zigzags. People walk on the streets with the cars as there are no good sidewalks.

Kabul, Afghanistan 2005
Masgue Pul Khishti Highway

Kabul, Afghanistan 2005

People walking on the street, and drivers driving down the street; this system is not good. The government is very lazy and 'doesn't have a good education. People with good educations and experience should run the government with a good system like America's. The Afghanistan government should encourage good education with good experience for jobs; people need jobs, housing, health, education, and security.

Afghanistan 2005 different location
1976 Kabul, Afghanistan (Jadi Miwand) on left on top line. Electric city buses were running during the civil wars after the communist government shut down and during President Dawood's administration. Electric buses were contracted with the government of Czechoslovakia and all electric buses have been destroyed.

Tower Ekhtyaruddin Castle at Heart Afghanistan
When the communist government was in power in Afghanistan, the Russian army took place at this location but Freedom Fighters in Heart gave them a good answer.

Kabul, Afghanistan 1976

The yellow building is Pashtani Business Bank, and the city bus is a Mercedes-Benz from Germany. The traffic system in Afghanistan from the beginning was not good and is still not good. I hope new government in Afghanistan can bring a better system for traffic in Afghanistan. Right now, the city buses are donated by Indian and Japanese governments.

Russian Jeep on the left and the tow bicycle riders on the street on Humber bicycles. The Rahil bicycle was famous in Afghanistan; it was made in England and expensive.

Our Life in **Afghanistan, Pakistan and the United States**

Shado Shamshira Mosque in central Kabul. People go five times a day to pray and celebrate their Islamic tradition. Famous mosque in Afghanistan and still to this day.

Mr. Abdul Wali, who lives in New Zealand, (Okland). The largest mosque and a famous place in Afghanistan, Mazar Sharrif can hold at one time more than 10,000 people for prayer and every year the first day of our New Year's on March 21. From all around Afghanistan people come for New Year's celebration.

People live in city locations. Their life becomes different. Better education, housing, and better jobs. In some parts of Afghanistan, the government pays no attention to them. There is no government office, no hospital, and no school; roads are not good and there is no good medical practice. If they get sick they travel by donkey or walk a day or two to go to the clinic and for doctor visits and to buy medicine. According to the people in towns, their people got sick and died. Because for some of them the economy was good enough to be able to go to town to visit the doctors or to buy medicine.

The village was big and more than 10,000 people were living there with no schools, and no electricity. Children need schools. Parents send the children out to collect wood and expect them to be able to cook bread and food. I asked some of the children, "You like school?" They told me, "We like to go to school, but we don't have schools." They ask me to teach them writing and reading.

I sat down on the ground with them to teach them. "Children need respect and need a good life, good education."

They were listening to every word I told them. "Children should be able to go to school." But they couldn't go to school because their fathers were planting and the children were out collecting wood. During the daytime, the children walk on and around the hills and mountains four or five miles and come back home. I asked these children where they bought the ruler. They told me their father bought it while in town. It was very hard for kids like these to not wear work shoes and have no gloves to collect wood from the mountains and hills.

Children with their donkey collecting wood from the mountain for their livelihood. They need better clothes. These children have never attended school. They need a better education and better transportation. I hope the Afghanistan government pays attention to these people's lives away from the capital or city.

Two of them have shoes and three of them have no shoes. They are walking and running on the hard ground on stone and their feet are like stone.

I want attention for the Afghanistan people. On the right we can see a small river. People get their drinking water from that river. Life is very hard for these children and their families.

Their fathers were busy during the daytime planning, and children were

Farid **Muti**

outside collecting some things for life. They walk or ride donkeys across all of the desert and mountains to go to town once a week or biweekly for shopping. Children told me they eat a small piece of bread and tea, and around three o'clock their family makes dough. The dough is made from yogurt and water mixed with a spoon or by hand and a drink. With no electricity, they have to do all things in the daytime, and when it gets dark, they sleep.

Afghan people like guests. They have an open house. No calls no appointments, you just go and visit and they provide lunch and dinner. They are happy for their culture and customs.

The children asked me many questions. One of many was "Where are you from?" The question was asked because I shaved daily and my accent was of the Dari language. Most of the children had a hat on, and Abdul Jabaar had on a turban. A turban was a tradition of the village.

During my travels, my attention was on these kids. The other kids didn't have good clothes and shoes to wear, but some families living at the village were rich, and their children rode motorcycles. The two boys here were 10 and 14 years old. Here around the village where they lived, they had no control over traffic. I asked them how they managed three kids on one motorcycle and were they going to school. They said they were not going to school. They said that in their village, they don't have schools, no teachers, no doctors, and no police.

I asked this boy how old he was and he told me 12 years old. I asked him if he was going to school and he told me no school. I asked him about his father and he said that his father had died a communist; Russia killed him.

The weather was cold here. I had on warm clothes. The children here looked happy with smiles, but during the cold weather, many of them wore big clothes, and a few had no coats nor warm clothes. All of them had hats and turbans on their heads.

When kids were collecting wood from the desert and mountains, one of them was with his father, and they had a goat and a small sheep. I told them I wanted to buy this goat. They told me it would be 1,500 Afghan, which is equal to 30 US dollars. I kept it for two weeks and after two weeks the goat died. Maybe the goat was upset from being away from the parents. I fed the goat well but we traveled a lot. The goat was tired going around the desert, hills, and mountains.

The people at the village take water for drinking and cooking from the river at the left of the picture. No schools, hospitals, or government, and the roads are not good. During the winter some of their homes are very cold. They don't have support for heating because the heating system that they use is not like the modern technology of America.

Life is different for everybody around the world. People's lives at the village

Our Life in **Afghanistan, Pakistan and the United States**

here in Afghanistan are different than the lives of people in the city section of Afghanistan. In the picture are senior people who live in the village. They have long gray beards. When I talked with them they told me that the Afghanistan government never pays attention to their town. Government comes and goes but it is not coming to work for their town to provide jobs. They are not concerned with building schools for their children or hospitals for them. When King Zahir Shah was there, no attention was paid.

After Zahir Shah in 1972, his cousin became president. His name was Moohd Dawood. The communist government came into power in 1928-1988 and 1989. No attention was paid then and still no attention now for their children and for their town.

The older people told me that they brought their drinking water from a small river. This is also where they washed their clothes, and the boys and men took showers in the river.

Some people travel by their camel or donkey to do business close to the city. They buy vegetables, sugar, salt, clothes, and other items for the village people. They go shopping in the city every month, sometimes twice a month. If people get sick and can not pay for rent to owner, they get on their camel and go to a different town to visit the doctor and hospital. They travel to different towns for two days or longer. One camel price in Afghanistan is 70,000 Afghani or 1,200 US dollars. The camel is good transportation and brings money for owner.

I talked with the chief of police. His office was five miles away from the village, which was very hard for older people, children, and women. I asked the chief of police, government, and representatives of the village why 'they didn't pay attention to the villages. They told me they don't have budgets and that the government is very poor and that everyone would have to take care of themselves. The chief of police told me that they don't even have uniforms. "If we cannot take care of the town government, how can we take care of the villages?" asked the chief of police. If the village did not belong to his religion, he didn't care.

Older people told me that if they didn't belong to them nor their religion, they don't care about the people who lived in the village. But after one week, the chief of police purchased 20 acres land for 40 thousand US dollars.

Middle: Farid Muti and right: Chief of Police, who has no uniform, and his soldiers had no uniforms. Later on we found out that the chief and his soldiers have never been to school and have no education. I asked the soldiers how much they get a month as salary from the government. They only get three meals, breakfast, lunch, and dinner. If the government gave a salary for the soldiers, the governor and chief of police and others kept it for themselves and shared amongst each other.

Government soldiers making a fire to keep warm. It was winter and very cold. I asked the soldiers to give me change for 100 Afghani. I asked them what they had and they told me they had Pakistani rupees. I told them, this is Afghanistan; shouldn't they have Afghani in their pockets? They told me if anyone asks, the governor or chief of police or others, they have Pakistani rupees.

These children were cold. During the winter, life is very different. The children don't have clothes for cold and freezing weather. No one cares about these children enough to think about their future. If we take care of these children and give them education and training for the future, they will be good doctors, engineers, scientists, or teachers for Afghanistan to help their people in their town and village.

Soldiers invited me for tea and hospitality. They were thinking I came from Kabul, Afghanistan. I was a Farsi speaker, but I talked with them and pushed them to speak both languages. They had a Russian teapot, which cost, in Kabul, 500 Afghani or ten US dollars. They were hobby for cultural and custom at their village. Each town and village in Afghanistan has different accents and different customs.

Governor John Mohd Afghanistan

When I talked with the governor about the village and about their problems, the governor paid no attention to the conversation. I told him he was the governor, and that he had a good home with a big generator and a bodyguard and a land cruiser. I told him he should stop to think about his people. He didn't have a good education, no schooling. During King, he was a doorman at the school. Why did he become governor? Because he was a friend of Hamid Karzai, President of Afghanistan. We had an appointment with the governor at his office at 11 a.m. When we went to his office, he came from his home to work at 11:30 a.m.

My last stop. The Buhristan Cinema in Kabul, Afghanistan.

In Kabul, all cinemas are open, with three shows, 1 p.m., 4 p.m., and 8 p.m. Indian, American, and Iranian movies show at this US cinema in Kabul.

Kabul University is active, open, and has more than 27,000 boys and 9,000 girls enrolled.

Going to school, people moved from Pakistan, Iran to Kabul. They rebuilt their property and made a business in Kabul. For one half of the day the children went

Our Life in **Afghanistan, Pakistan and the United States**

to school and the other half they worked with their parents at home or outside. I saw teenagers selling phone cards in the market. I visited a video center where I purchased DVDs and a CD. The price of a CD was 50 Afghani, which equals one dollar US; DVDs were 85 Afghani, or $1.70 US. In the video center a father and son were working and his son was only ten years old. He gave the price of CD and DVD to pack back to the U.S.A.

Life in the capital was different. People lived like in the United States. The government people worn uniforms and dresses. Boys and girls going to school wore uniforms. Colleges and universities had an open dress policy. You could also choose the college you wanted to attend just by passing the college test.

CHAPTER**FIVE**
Children in Afghanistan and Children in Ameria

Groceries in Afghanistan

Each country has different rules. The United States of America has different rules than Europe, Germany, Sweden, Norway, Denmark, France, Canada, and England. If someone wants to run a business, they would have to have a business license from the state or local government. If they want a business inside of a shopping center where there is air-conditioning or a heating system, it's clean and also has restrooms. They also have computers and cash registers, and people have access to debit and credit cards or cash. In Afghanistan, if someone wants to run a business, he can do so without a license, but the law has to be followed. Most stores in Afghanistan are small. Kabul is the capital. Businessmen build large shopping centers. But unlike the American people, they use cash. They keep it in their wallets and pocket the cash. They do not use credit cards. Everyone thinks 'in terms of cash. If someone doesn't have money and the owner of the shop knows him, he can buy his stuff and the owner will make a note of how much he bought and the date. Later, the customer should pay the money back. If he 'doesn't pay it back, the owner will not be happy to see to him or sell him things from his store.

It is not necessary that grocery or shopping centers have restrooms. In the big shopping centers there are maybe one or two restrooms that all the shop owners can use. When people go to buy their vegetables, they should have with them paper or plastic bags, and some families have cloth bags. Kids collect papers like magazines and newspapers and sell them to the stores for four to ten cents per pound. The owner of the store makes paper packets for his business.

When I was a kid we bought our fresh vegetables from the vegetable store, which was close to our house, and we bought other stuff like rice, beans, salt, sugar, oil, and dry goods. My father shopped in town once a month and saved it at home. In Afghanistan, a monthly salary is not every week or bimonthly like in America. People who are employed by the government have good benefits, health insurance, and food assistance, and employers pay a small membership fee for the government. All employees in Afghanistan receive their salary monthly in cash. Forty hours per week is not hourly work in Afghanistan. The Afghanistan government pays a monthly salary in cash for each employee.

While my family and I were shopping, I saw my elementary school teacher from 30 years ago. I told my wife and she asked if I was sure. My wife said let's ask, so we did. I asked her if she was a schoolteacher at Jamal Mina Elementary School, Kabul, Afghanistan in 1972, and she replied yes. Her name was Adellah Tokhi. We introduced our families and until this day, we are like a big family.

There were so many houses around our school. Because of the private home, the government made a contract with the owner of the house to make it a school building. The school had 12 classrooms and a large office. All of the teachers and headmasters sat together, but there was no principal. The middle schools didn't have a library, labs, or a playground. The high schools had libraries, labs, a soccer field, and volleyball and basketball courts.

From 1972-2005 there were no changes in elementary schools. I didn't see any change from the government.

When you go to purchase a kilogram of meat from the butcher shop, all shops have scales that have one side for meats and the other side a kilogram weight they made from rock. But there is no way of telling the actual weight of the rock. Sometimes it's less than a kilogram. We are not patriots. If we were patriots why would Afghanistan allow this situation. We should know our duty.

All shops and stores put their stuff for sale outside of their shops, which was against the law. But no one controlled the law. Today a one-kilogram onion is 50 Afghanis, or one US dollar, which is one day's salary for a clerk in Afghanistan.

One kilogram of grapes 100 Afghanis = $2
One kilogram of apples 80 Afghanis = $1.80
Meat one kilogram 250 Afghanis = $5
Tomatoes one kilogram 50 Afghanis = $1
Eggplant one kilogram 40 Afghanis = 80 cents

Once a week on Friday, we have a Juma Bazaar; in English it's a Friday Bazaar. Vegetables, meat, clothes, and other items can be purchased at lower prices. All of the businesses bring their crops to this place, which was chosen by the government. On Friday is our weekend holiday government. The week is from Saturday to 1 p.m. on Thursday. From Thursday at 1 p.m. to Saturday at 8 a.m.,

Our Life in **Afghanistan, Pakistan and the United States**

the government is in Afghanistan.

Urozgan, Afghanistan

On Friday some people go shopping in town. Some of them are going to picnic with their family and friends. It is the tradition of Afghan during the holiday and Friday to fly kite's and have dog fights. Again, the government chose the location for the people.

Different size kites/names

1. Nim Takhtaee
2. 3 Parcha
3. 5 Parcha
4. 7 Parcha
5. Patangak
6. Mayeecha
7. Chanzapolyee Kak

Rich people during summer and spring spend special holidays and weekends in Jalal Abad from Kabul, 120 miles away from Kabul capital.

Urozgan, Afghanistan

At the Friday Bazaar, people came from 15 miles away by walking or by riding bicycles and motorcycles. The Bazaar was famous. We could see children coming in town without any shoes or warm clothes. They walked on hard ground with rocks and broken glass. It was very hard for them. I did not see traffic or police in the town. Kids were looking around. The boy in the picture had on his right shoulder a bag for his items he purchased in town.

Kids helped their parents in business. These kids need better freedom and better democracy. If they stay behind in the shop, it is better to go to school to learn to be somebody for the future. I asked their father how many kids he had and he told me four boys and two daughters. He had two daughters at home with his wife helping their mother around the home. He said that the area in which they lived didn't have schools so he opened a shop without a license. He had no electricity and had to have light by candles or hand lamps. He said that after 4 p.m. the shops closed and everyone went home. The man's name was Abdul Hamid and his children's names were Abdul, Hakim, Saboor, Rashid, and

Farid**Muti**

Wassy. I asked Abdul to tell me about his memories and experience at his job. He told me a very sad story.

"A year ago one young and strong boy, who was twenty-five years old, bought a cucumber from the vegetable store. He started to eat it. Another boy who was close by asked him for the cucumber and tried forcing him to give the cucumber to him. He was defiant, and a fight started between the two boys. Everybody told them not to fight and they were very ugly. The guy eating his cucumber was Kalil and he killed Jalil with a big knife. Kalil's relatives were shopping around when they found Kalil killed by the other guy. They found Jalil and started fighting. Jalil was very strong and a was a heavyweight champion boxer in the area. Kalil's relatives were three people, and Jalil killed three of them over one cucumber. Altogehter, Jalil killed four people. Everybody was very upset in our village and very quiet but Jalil skipped town, and we don't know where he is. His family is looking for Jalil. Jalil's family and the victim's family are enemies."

He told me other sad stories. "On October 16, 2003, American doctors were in our town to check up on our people and give medicine. The American medical group checked all of the children, old, young, and anybody who was sick. They gave them medicine for better health. A father named Durani brought his daughter because she was sick. The sickness was tuberculosis. Doctors gave medicine and advice for her father. They told him to give her the medicine and we gave them $200 (10200 Afghanis) to take her to the local hospital in town. The father said okay but was dishonest and he was not faithful with his family and daughter. He kept the money. He spent all the money gambling, smoking, and drinking. He didn't care about his daughter's sickness, and every day she was more sick because the medicine the American's gave her had run out. The American medical group had moved around the country to help other villages but later she died. She lost her life because her father was a demagogue."

I was trying to leave him to see more people, but he gave one last story.

"Four months ago in our neighborhood there was a wedding party, with the bride and groom and their family. They invited friends and relatives. Between the groom's family with other family was a tormenter. All were happy to participate in this happy celebration and the bride and groom were happy that everyone could come and celebrate. Their family was unhappy with the groom's family but mother and daughter were happy to go to the wedding party. Her husband protested. He told his wife and mother-in-law, 'We are not going to participate with these kind of people.The mother and daughter and other relatives participated at the wedding party. When he came home, no one was home. He was upset and didn't know where they were. He became nervous and superior.

Our Life in **Afghanistan, Pakistan and the United States**

When they came back from the wedding, he asked his wife and mother-in-law where they had been. They told him they went to the wedding party. The mother-in-law told him, 'My son, listen to their family. Forget it. They invited us to the wedding. Me and your wife went with other relatives. We went to the party.He was very nervous and ugly. He hit his mother-in-law with a punch. His wife told him to take it easy. 'She is my mother. You don't have respect for my mother and me.The husband and wife started fighting each other. He was out of control. He hit his wife very hard by his hand and punched her. He killed his wife because she went with her mother to a wedding party. He went to a Mosque and learned Quran and reading and writing there. Everyone in this town were upset and they were not happy. They needed help from the Afghanistan government to help their people for a better life. Children should go to school and we should have hospitals and clinics in our town."

I am 42 years old and in all of my life I have remembered the government in Afghanistan not helping and 'not caring about our town and our people.

The two tractor men were named Kahlid Khans and Jamal Khan. They were working at their farms from 6 a.m. through 5 p.m. They had a very old tractor with an unsafe body and overloaded it on unsafe roads. I asked them if people had bicycles in this town. "People don't have food to eat but you two have a tractor." The truck belonged to their father, who taught them how to operate it, but he passed away and left it for them. I asked him if the government gave them permission to drive the tractor and he said he didn't have a license. They were asked where they bought gas to drive and they said every weekend they go to town to buy their gas. The tractor man and his friend looked smarter than other people in town. Both tractor men put on their mount (nas) made from tobacco, but stronger than cigarettes and not good for their health and appetite. Both men had black turbans, custom-made clothes, and both were unsafe, no work shoes, no work or safety gloves, no safety glasses. Most of the farmers in Afghanistan don't have these safety materials. We don't have safe laws in Afghanistan. I asked the two men if they knew their governor, John Mohd, Chief of Police in Ullah and told them they were coming to visit the town and people at this village. They told me they were not coming to visit them. They didn't know them. I asked them about the government and President Karzai and his cabinet. They said, "Oh my brother, they only care about themselves. They don't care about people's lives and Afghanistan." They were not satisfied with the government. Each government was not in control of Afghanistan. They didn't work for the people. They brought more fratricide between people. We want that government to bring equal rights and reasoning and bring justice to Afghanistan. I am in agreement with the two men. I am happy for equal rights

Farid **Muti**

and justice in Afghanistan. Some people have millions of dollars and others don't have lunch or dinner to eat and their children don't have shoes and proper clothing.

It is not easy. But life is good for everybody. Everybody around the world wants a better life and better communities and to have good jobs, cars, and homes. But not him. He is walking on the thistly ground. His feet were like a porcupine or hedgehog and very hard. He didn't feel a piece of glass or rock or thistle on the ground. He was running, walking around like others. I saw more boys and girls walking and running on the ground of thistles and motes and echinoidea. The two boys came close to me and they asked me for pen and a notebook. I asked them what their names were. One told me Abdul Malik and the other Autaullah. I asked if they were going to school and they told me no. They said they didn't have schools. They were going to the Mosque to learn Quran and learn to read Alpabeth. They were able to write their names with a promise to give them a pencil and notebook to each of them. They were very smart and good listeners and cheerful. They asked me if I could teach them how to read and write. I told them with much gladness, yes. I told them that I taught English reading and writing to Afghan refugee's from 1985-1991 when I was a refugee in Pakistan. Both were happy for a half hour. They laughed and ran around on the thistly ground.

People around the world live in different ways, with different cultures and customs. The clothes the boys had on were from their culture and their customs in that town. Our children go around town with dress shirt and pants. All the people look on with surprise and wonder where they came from. Abdul Malik and Autaullah were sitting on humid ground learning something and other children were running on sandy regions. But in the winter, the weather is very cold, rainy and sometimes snowing. The children still continue daily activities of walking and running. And in the hot summer they walk on combustible, burning ground.

Abdul Malik and Autaullah father's died when the Russian army was in Afghanistan. Neither of them saw' their father's face at death. They were very diehard, heartbroken. Their life has been difficult. Most Afghan children are oppressed. They are in need of commendation from UN, Europe, the U.S. and around the world.

Since 1960 to today, I have experienced the Afghanistan government. During King Zahee Shah's reign of 40 years, his cousin Mohd Dawood (Sarddar) started a revolution in 1972. He became President of our King Shah Zahee. He was in Italy for his vacation. In 1978 the communist government took control of Afghanistan. After the communists, the Mujahideen took control of Afghanistan and the Taliban. None of them helped the children to go to school or to even build schools. We could not find any educated people at their villages in Urozgan, Afghanistan.

Our Life in **Afghanistan, Pakistan and the United States**

Figure 1

Farid**Muti**

Figure 2

Our Life in **Afghanistan, Pakistan and the United States**

Figure 3

Farid**Muti**

Figure 4

Figure 5

Farid**Muti**

Figure 6

WAKE TECHNICAL COMMUNITY COLLEGE

3 3063 00150778 8

Wake Tech. Libraries
9101 Fayetteville Road
Raleigh, North Carolina 27603-5696

WN DATE DUE

GAYLORD   PRINTED IN U.S.A.

AUG '02

Printed in the United States
105374LV00004B/1-100/A

9 781432 715274